30-Day Devotional
Your Tongue Is Writing Your Destiny!

Proverbs 18:21
Death and life are in the power of the tongue, and those who love it will eat its fruits.

Written by Ebony Vaz

Copyright 2024 by Ebony Vaz
All Scriptures are from the English Standard Version (ESV) Bible

Table of Contents

Introduction ....

Instructions ....

Day 1 1

   The words you speak..

Day 2 3

   Helping your words become a blessing to others ....

Day 3 5

   Words are a tool ....

Day 4 7

   Blank Check..

Day 5 9

   Renew your mind..

Day 6 11

   Victory is in your words...

Day 7 13

   Shift your atmosphere ....

Day 8 15

   Angels or Demons...

Day 9 17

   Things above..

Day 10...19

Words are seeds...

Day 11 21
Your words have fruit ....

Day 12 23
Your words matter ....

Day 13 25
Your words can make you or break you ....

Day 14 27
What are your words giving access to? ....

Day 15 29
Your words are working for you ....

Day 16 31
Careless words ....

Day 17 33
Guard your mouth ....

Day 18 35
Send the word ....

Day 19 37
Established ....

Day 20 39
Responsible lips ....

Day 21 41

A quiet spirit..

Day 22..43

　Shining stars..

Day 23..45

　Slow to speak...

Day 24..47

　What is in your hands...

Day 25.. 49

　Your heart ....

Day 26 51

　Complaining..

Day 27..53

　Imagination ....

Day 28 55

　Don't let go..

Day 29 57

　Praise the Lord..

Day 30 59

　Testify ....

Reflections 61

My Prayer 🙏.. 62

Your Prayer 🙏... 64

Thank You 65

Introduction

I wrote this devotional because, growing up, people called me out of my name. I was picked on with words, which hurt me. Even though we say, "Sticks and stones may break my bones, but words will never hurt me," I felt hurt inside. Now that I'm older, I realize how powerful words are.

As I pray and read the Bible, it helps me watch what comes out of my mouth. Our words represent us and shape the worlds' perception of us. We should think before we talk because out of the heart the mouth speaks. Your words can carry you to amazing places, but only if you let them.

Let me help you on this 30-day journey to allow your words to lead you to your destiny and not destruction.

Instructions

STEP 1:
Each day for 30 days, read the devotional. Study and meditate on the scriptures that have been given.

STEP 2:
At the bottom of each page, there is a Reflections space. When done reading, write down what you have learned and how you will apply it to your life.

STEP 3:
When finished with the devotional, write your testimony and your biggest takeaways.

Remember to go back and use this as a tool for your everyday life.

Day 1

The words you speak

God has given us one of the most powerful tools on this earth: our tongue. The words that come out of our mouths can be blessings or curses. Your words will affect the outcome of your day and your life. Your words are a force; they have the power to express and communicate, to influence certain outcomes in your life. You can create the most beautiful dreams, or you can destroy everything around you. God has given us everything by speaking it into existence, so let us do the same for our everyday lives.

Scriptures:
James 3:10
From the same mouth come blessing and cursing. My brothers, these things ought not to be so.

Romans 4:17,18
As it is written, "I have made you the father of many nations"—in the presence of the God in whom he believed,

who gives life to the dead and calls into existence the things that do not exist.

In hope he believed against hope, that he should become the father of many nations, as he had been told, "So shall your offspring be."

Reflections: After reading today's devotion, how will you apply this to your life?

_____

_____

_____

Day 2

Helping your words become a blessing to others

Sometimes we can use words without thinking, but we can't think without using words. Encouraging words can save someone's life.

When you talk, don't focus on negativity; speak positive words toward one another, words people need to hear so they can grow stronger.

What you say can help build self-esteem in others. You can be a blessing to those who are listening.

Example: Your friend is having a bad day.

Positive words: ("Keep pushing") ("Storms don't last forever") ("You can do all things through Christ who strengthens you")

Scriptures:

Ephesians 4:29
Let no corrupting talk come out of your mouths, but only such as is good for building up, as fits the occasion, that it may give grace to those who hear.

1 Thessalonians 5:11
Therefore encourage one another and build one another up, just as you are doing.

Reflections: What are some encouraging words you can use today toward someone?

Day 3

Words are a tool

When we allow God to use us, he can do amazing things through us. Just as God uses physical tools to help humans, he also uses spiritual tools. God uses prayer as a tool to help us communicate with him. He also uses his Word as a tool to teach us about himself, but one thing I've realized is that faith is one of the most important tools to have.

Let us be careful not to waver; the Bible says that the just shall live by faith. We need to remain steadfast in our walk with God. We have all the tools we need to defeat the enemy.

Scriptures:
Philippians 4:6,7
Do not be anxious about anything, but in everything by prayer and supplication with thanksgiving let your requests be made known to God. And the peace of God, which surpasses all understanding, will guard your hearts and your minds in Christ Jesus.

2 Timothy 3:16,17

All Scripture is breathed out by God and profitable for teaching, for reproof, for correction, and for training in righteousness, that the man of God may be complete, equipped for every good work.

Reflections: What are three spiritual tools that would help you in your day-to-day life?

Examples: Music, Meditation, Prayer

1.
_____
2.
_____
3.
_____

Day 4

Blank Check

God gave you a blank check when were born. You can pursue every possibility, every opportunity, and every authority and possess freedom to walk in his plan for your future.

God has given us gifts and talents, physical and spiritual, for us to use what has been given to fill in the blanks of our checks.

We must think big and believe big because our God is a big God. He doesn't want us to think little of ourselves. God put something extraordinary and unique inside all of us and he doesn't want us to waste it.

Motivate yourself by speaking great things over your life, family, career, and workplace. Use your gifts, talents, skills, and ability to work hard so you can reap the benefits of your hard work.

Scriptures:

Colossians 3:23,24
Whatever you do, work heartily, as for the Lord and not for men, knowing that from the Lord you will receive the inheritance as your reward. You are serving the Lord Christ.

Ecclesiastes 3:12,13
I perceived that there is nothing better for them than to be joyful and to do good as long as they live; also that everyone should eat and drink and take pleasure in all his toil—this is God's gift to man.

Reflections: If you had a blank check in front of you and were able to fill in your life's desires, what would you do with it?

_____

_____

_____

Day 5

Renew your mind

Do not conform any longer to the patterns of this world, but be transformed by the renewing of your mind. You can do this by:

First, start your day with God. Then, meditate on his word and promises. When you meditate on God's word and his promises, it will help you remember you can do what God says you can do. You can have what God says you can have. You are who God says you are. You will begin to believe and say it in faith every day. This will help you put on your new self, created after the likeness of God in true righteousness and holiness.

Having the right mindset will help you clear your mind from any anxiety, fear, worry, and doubt you may have from this world. Remember, God said to be in the world, but not of the world. He has overcome the world.

Scriptures:
Romans 12:2

Do not be conformed to this world, but be transformed by the renewal of your mind, that by testing you may discern what is the will of God, what is good and acceptable and perfect.

Mark 9:23
And Jesus said to him, "'If you can'! All things are possible for one who believes."

Reflections: What do you need to change regarding your mindset?

_____

_____

_____

Day 6

Victory is in your words

Don't worry about what you see; focus on what God is saying. Your words carry emotions and feelings. The more positive words you say each day can compel you to act and influence the decisions you make about life, both large and small. Never let your mouth agree with fleeting emotions.

If you feel down, speak life over your situation because we have the victory! God wants you to make your intentions and desires known.

Along with prayer about your desires, remember that faith without works is dead. Faith is believing even when you don't see it happening. For the Lord, your God, is the one who goes with you to fight for you against your enemies to give you victory.

Example: (When your classmates or coworkers are talking about you)

You: "It's okay, because God has the last say, and he fights my battles for me."

Scriptures:
Romans 4:17
As it is written, "I have made you the father of many nations"—in the presence of the God in whom he believed, who gives life to the dead and calls into existence the things that do not exist.

Philippians 4:13
I can do all things through him who strengthens me.

Reflections: What would you say to change a bad situation into a good situation?

_____

_____

_____

Day 7

Shift your atmosphere

When it looks impossible, you must begin to praise God in the midst of the storm. Many of the things we live through are testing our maturity and faith. God wants us to be steadfast, well-balanced and immovable regardless of what's going on around us.

You can shift your atmosphere by focusing on what God has done for you, because if he did it before he will do it again. Go out and do the things that make you happy. Set your mind on things above and not earthly things. Shift your mindset and the way you think. Keep positive and uplifting people around you who will motivate you.

You got this!

Example: I will not worry because God will keep me in perfect peace.

Scriptures:
Isaiah 41:10

Fear not, for I am with you; be not dismayed, for I am your God; I will strengthen you, I will help you, I will uphold you with my righteous right hand.

John 16:13
When the Spirit of truth comes, he will guide you into all the truth, for he will not speak on his own authority, but whatever he hears he will speak, and he will declare to you the things that are to come.

Reflections: What are the ways you can change the atmosphere in your home?

_____

_____

_____

Day 8

Angels or Demons

Do you give power to angels or demons? When you speak, angels are listening, but the enemy is as well. Angels are sent by God to protect us and help us inherit his full kingdom. The Bible tells us that angels are his servants carrying out his will. They work for our good. Angels are ministering spirits sent to serve those who have salvation. They intervene on behalf of humans. Whose side are you leaning on? Light excels all darkness. Put your trust in God and speak his word.

Scriptures:
Psalm 103:20
Bless the LORD, O you his angels, you mighty ones who do his word, obeying the voice of his word!

Psalm 91:11
For he will command his angels concerning you to guard you in all your ways.

Reflections: If an angel appeared at your bedside, what would you say or do?

_____

_____

_____

Day 9

Things above

Set your thoughts and affections on heavenly things instead of worldly things. Too often our minds are consumed with children, bills, jobs, school, and other things which can cause stress.

When our mind is set on Heaven and not on earth which is temporary, we are able to focus on the things that are important, like our relationship with God and others. When our minds are filled with the truth of the Bible, we know what God says about us. We are better equipped to make wise decisions and live in a way that pleases God. Keeping your mind stayed on heavenly things will help you not to sin.

When we set our eyes on Him, we are better able to serve him and service is the duty and pleasure of an everyday believer. A heavenly mindset teaches us to define our identity not by the person we see in the mirror, but by the Savior we see in scripture.

Scriptures:

Colossians 3:2

Set your minds on things that are above, not on things that are on earth.

Psalm 119:11

I have stored up your word in my heart, that I might not sin against you.

Reflections: How can you live heavenly minded?

Day 10

Words are seeds

You can plant seeds with your words. They have the power to build or destroy. Anything that has seeds has the ability to bring forth fruit.

By not allowing negative words to come out of your mouth toward yourself or others, you help water seeds without pulling up the roots.

When words are spoken, they can settle in a person's soul. Words grow and can produce something great either in you or someone else. Wise words satisfy like a good meal; the right words bring satisfaction. The word of God is like a seed that must be planted and nourished so that it may bloom in due season.

Scriptures:
Matthew 13:19
When anyone hears the word of the kingdom and does not understand it, the evil one comes and snatches away what

has been sown in his heart. This is what was sown along the path.

Matthew 13:23
As for what was sown on good soil, this is the one who hears the word and understands it. He indeed bears fruit and yields, in one case a hundredfold, in another sixty, and in another thirty."

Reflections: What are some words you can plant inside yourself or others that will keep growing?

Day 11

Your words have fruit

If you want the results of something good and prosperous in your life, you must let your words be of good fruit. You can't talk defeat and expect victory. You can't talk lack and expect to have abundance. We will eat the fruit of our words, so make sure your words are inspiring you and the people you love. Words give life, joy, peace and love, so be a person who makes a difference. If you don't have Jesus in your life, you will never bear fruit.

Scriptures:
Matthew 12:33
"Either make the tree good and its fruit good, or make the tree bad and its fruit bad, for the tree is known by its fruit.

Galatians 5:22,23
But the fruit of the Spirit is love, joy, peace, patience, kindness, goodness, faithfulness, gentleness, self-control; against such things there is no law.

Reflections: What is your favorite fruit and how would you describe it?

_____

_____

_____

Day 12

Your words matter

The words we choose convey our thoughts and feelings. Words can hurt, offend, and provoke, but they can also empower, uplift, and inspire. Words have so much influence that they can cause a person's life to change.

Words have the power of life when we share the good news of Christ with others and encourage fellow believers. Sharing kind words, healing words, affirming words with each other can bring people together.

The words we speak toward one another can help people see themselves better than they are feeling. You are in control of the words that come out of your mouth! Speak what you would want someone say to you.

Scriptures:
Proverbs 10:19
When words are many, transgression is not lacking, but whoever restrains his lips is prudent.

Proverbs 8:6
Hear, for I will speak noble things, and from my lips will come what is right,

Reflections: What words can you use to uplift yourself while looking in the mirror?

_____

_____

_____

Day 13

Your words can make you or break you

Your words can lead you to success or failure. You decide whether to win with your words or lose with your words. Let your words uplift you in a way no one can bring you down. Words can't hurt you without your permission. When you know who you are, words can't break you!

Let negative words pass by like the wind. Your words can shatter dreams or energize them. Words are like throwing a stone in the ocean, but do you have any idea how deep that stone can go?

Scriptures:
1 Corinthians 13:1
If I speak in the tongues of men and of angels, but have not love, I am a noisy gong or a clanging cymbal.

Proverbs 18:4
The words of a man's mouth are deep waters; the fountain of wisdom is a bubbling brook.

Reflections: What are some kind words you can say to someone having a bad day?

_____

_____

_____

Day 14

What are your words giving access to?

Think about what you're speaking over your life. Before you speak, ask the Holy Spirit to give you the words to say. The doorway to your words lets in light; let that light give wisdom, revelation, and understanding to the inexperienced.

Let the light of your words touch the listener's heart and soul. God loves when we build each other up so let your words unfold miracles that can bring someone back to life.

Scriptures:
Psalm 119:130
The unfolding of your words gives light; it imparts understanding to the simple.

Proverbs 18:6,7
A fool's lips walk into a fight, and his mouth invites a beating. A fool's mouth is his ruin, and his lips are a snare to his soul.

Reflections: Why should we watch our words?

_____

_____

_____

Day 15

Your words are working for you

Let your words work as hard as you do! Let your words carry your day in a positive way. Our good words become the moment of God's grace in the lives of others. Our words should be full of positivity.

Waking up in the morning, we should thank God he woke us up, and say to ourselves, "This is going to be the best day ever because I am in it," and make your words work for you. Set your day off the right way by encouraging yourself.

Scriptures:
Ephesians 5:6
Let no one deceive you with empty words, for because of these things the wrath of God comes upon the sons of disobedience.

Jeremiah 15:16

Your words were found, and I ate them, and your words became to me a joy and the delight of my heart, for I am called by your name, O LORD, God of hosts.

Reflections: What are some ways you can put your words into action?

_____

_____

_____

Day 16

Careless words

On the day of judgment, you will have to give an account of every careless word you have spoken. The careless words you speak say a lot about who you are on the inside.

Jesus reminds us in Matthew 12:34, "For out of the abundance of the heart the mouth speaks." Our words often say more about us than we realize. Your words reveal your character. Your words should bless rather than curse and uplift rather than tear down.

Instead of gossip and slander, change your heart to speak words of hope and love. Keep your mouth in check! Sometimes it's better to say nothing at all.

Scriptures:
Matthew 12:36,37
I tell you, on the day of judgment people will give account for every careless word they speak, for by your words you will be justified, and by your words you will be condemned."

Proverbs 12:18,19

There is one whose rash words are like sword thrusts, but the tongue of the wise brings healing. Truthful lips endure forever, but a lying tongue is but for a moment.

Reflections: What are some careless words you have used?

_____

_____

_____

Day 17

Guard your mouth

"He who guards his lips, guards his life, but he who speaks rashly will come to ruin (Proverbs 13:3). Because our words are valuable and powerful, when we speak, we need to ask God to guide our mouth. In doing that, we're acknowledging the importance of saying what we mean and meaning what we say. Guarding your mouth keeps you out of trouble! Watching what comes out of your mouth will help you in many ways.

What you say gives an excellent reading of the condition of your heart spiritually. Think before you speak and you will go a long way in life.

Scriptures:
Proverbs 21:23
Whoever keeps his mouth and his tongue keeps himself out of trouble.

Philippians 2:14,15
Do all things without grumbling or disputing,

that you may be blameless and innocent, children of God without blemish in the midst of a crooked and twisted generation, among whom you shine as lights in the world,

Reflections: When is a time you should have guarded your mouth but didn't? What did you learn from it?

_____

_____

_____

Day 18

Send the word

In the Bible, God sent the word and people were healed. Miracles, signs and wonders happened because God sent the word and God's words don't come back void or empty. Let the words you speak set you free from addictions, poverty, temptations and worry. Encouraging words can help you start your day off right and bright. It will help you strengthen your faith in every situation in life.

God sent his word, so put yourself in a position to receive it. Let his words elevate you and meet your needs. His word is his wisdom! It is the Holy Spirit who directs us to and through his word.

If you're in pain, send the word of healing to your pain. God has given us power and authority to trample over the enemy (Luke 10:19). Let us speak the word over everything that is holding us back!

Scriptures:

Psalm 107:20
He sent out his word and healed them, and delivered them from their destruction.

Isaiah 55:11
So shall my word be that goes out from my mouth; it shall not return to me empty, but it shall accomplish that which I purpose, and shall succeed in the thing for which I sent it.

Reflections: What word would you send forth to change your situation?

_____

_____

_____

Day 19

Established

The Lord is faithful, and he will establish, strengthen, grow, confirm and multiply every area of your life. God anointed us and established us in Christ. The spirit of God is in our hearts, a seal that is our guarantee of eternal life.

Align your words with the word of God commit to the Lord, whatever you do.

Job 22:28-29 says, "You will decide on a matter, and it will be established for you, and light will shine on your ways. For when they are humbled you say, 'It is because of pride'; but he saves the lowly."

Scriptures:
1 Kings 8:20
Now the LORD has fulfilled his promise that he made. For I have risen in the place of David my father, and sit on the throne of Israel, as the LORD promised, and I have built the house for the name of the LORD, the God of Israel.

1 Corinthians 1:8
Who will sustain you to the end, guiltless in the day of our Lord Jesus Christ.

Reflections: Are the words you're speaking establishing something in your future?

_____

_____

_____

Day 20

Responsible lips

Being responsible with your lips will help God protect you. Oil flows from those who are responsible with their lips. If God said life and death are in the tongue, how can God use you if your tongue is filthy? Your spirit must align with your lips. Let your lips be used for praising God, being thankful, and good use. Close your lips If you have nothing good to say toward someone.

Don't let your lips look better than how you speak. The instrument of deliverance is in your lips, so let what you speak be purposeful.

Scriptures:
Psalm 141:3
Set a guard, O LORD, over my mouth; keep watch over the door of my lips!

Psalm 51:15
O Lord, open my lips, and my mouth will declare your praise.

Reflections: How can you be responsible with your lips?

_____

_____

_____

Day 21

A quiet spirit

Your beauty shouldn't come from outward adornment, but it should come from your inner self. Before you begin to form judgments toward someone, remember it's only by God's grace that you're where you are today. A meek and quiet spirit is one of the greatest prizes in the sight of God.

Learn to be quiet so your words can establish good things. Be of a calm and quiet spirit and God will turn things in your favor. Having a quiet and calm spirit will help you feel secure in the Lord. Quietness will help you discern God's hand in the work of your enemies. Being quiet is priceless.

Scriptures:
1 Peter 3:3,4
Do not let your adorning be external—the braiding of hair and the putting on of gold jewelry, or the clothing you wear— but let your adorning be the hidden person of the

heart with the imperishable beauty of a gentle and quiet spirit, which in God's sight is very precious.

Matthew 5:5
Blessed are the meek, for they shall inherit the earth.

Reflections: Try sometime this week to have a quiet and meek spirit. Try to listen without talking. Time yourself for twenty minutes. See how much of a difference it makes. Write down your experience.

_____

_____

_____

Day 22

Shining stars

Let us be a star that is guided by the lord. Shining stars have a light that shines so brightly they cannot be dimmed. Each star has a name that God has given it. "We are that star!"

Be a star that is wise and guides people to Jesus. God wants us to be light in this dark world; a star that goes above and beyond to bring brightness to another person's day.

God cares about us. We matter to him far beyond the stars. He knows our needs and reads our hearts. Be a star that cannot be hidden. You are unique, made to be set aside and different. You were made to shine!

Scriptures:
Psalm 147:4
He determines the number of the stars; he gives to all of them their names.

Daniel 12:3

And those who are wise shall shine like the brightness of the sky above; and those who turn many to righteousness, like the stars forever and ever.

Reflections: When you look up into the nighttime sky and see the stars, what comes to mind?

_____

_____

_____

Day 23

Slow to speak

Don't just hear the word; be a doer of the word! When you listen more than you talk, growth happens. Listening helps us to live in ways marked by patience and peace. Allow God to transform you as he leads you in the way of righteousness.

As children of God, we should be quick to listen, slow to speak, and slow to become angry. Doing it God's way is the better way to live and reflect true faith and obedience to Christ. We must be thoughtful in our speaking and display wisdom as we are listening so that when we talk it is the Holy Spirit speaking through us.

Scriptures:
James 1:19,20
Know this, my beloved brothers: let every person be quick to hear, slow to speak, slow to anger; for the anger of man does not produce the righteousness of God.

Titus 3:2

To speak evil of no one, to avoid quarreling, to be gentle, and to show perfect courtesy toward all people.

Reflections: When was a time you were quick to anger, and you didn't listen to the person first? How would you do it differently this time around?

_____

_____

_____

Day 24

What is in your hands

God always uses what we have in our hands. God will use what he has given you. Whenever God comes to a person, he will ask you what is in your hands to see if you are conscious of what he has placed in you.

In the Bible (Exodus 4:1-5), God told Moses to lead the children of Israel into the promised land, but Moses was afraid. God asked him what is in your hand? To Moses, it was just a rod, but to God it was the instrument by which miracles would be performed.

Many times, we look outside ourselves for help to do something. This is doubting God's ability to use what he placed in you. God wants us to take the little and make it into something more than enough for us. Everything you do will have an impact on your life.

Scriptures:
1 Timothy 4:14

Do not neglect the gift you have, which was given you by prophecy when the council of elders laid their hands on you.

1 Thessalonians 4:11
And to aspire to live quietly, and to mind your own affairs, and to work with your hands, as we instructed you,

Reflections: What has God placed in you? What gifts and talents has God given you to use?

_____

_____

_____

Day 25

Your heart

Make sure your heart is aligned with God's will and purpose for your life. Don't let your heart be troubled. Don't despise what you have now. Instead, be grateful for it. Nurture it with all your heart and speak the word of God into it. Then watch God use it to increase you.

Let God cleanse your heart. If it is not in right standing with God, ask him for a new heart that is acceptable to him. Loving, sweet, grateful hearts can touch the heart of Jesus. Once God has your heart, he can guide and direct you in every area of your life.

Scriptures:
John 14:1
Let not your hearts be troubled. Believe in God; believe also in me.

Proverbs 4:23
Keep your heart with all vigilance, for from it flow the springs of life.

Reflections: How is your heart? Is there anything you need to change or remove?

_____

_____

_____

Day 26

Complaining

Nothing happens by chance. You are in your situation for a reason and a season. It's all part of God's plan and it will work together for your good, but that can only happen if you stop despising and complaining. Don't complain about what you have and start seeing what God wants to do through it. Praise God for what you have, and what he has done for you!

The more you complain the more death sets in. There are no successful complainers. We must have joy in our souls. You can't control what's beyond you. Give God a chance to come in and help your situation. Let it bring you closer to him. Give God full control of everything in your life. You will start to see what you have is more than enough!

Scriptures:
Numbers 11:1
And the people complained in the hearing of the LORD about their misfortunes, and when the LORD heard it, his

anger was kindled, and the fire of the LORD burned among them and consumed some outlying parts of the camp.

Psalm 150:6
Let everything that has breath praise the LORD! Praise the LORD!

Reflections: Instead of complaining about your situation, what can you do to make it better?

_____

_____

_____

Day 27

Imagination

Imagination invites us to breathe, dream, and to be fully present to the wonder of it all. Imagination is powerful because it can influence everything we do, think and create. It could be big and good, or it could be wild and bad. It's up to us.

To imagine is to form something not present and bring it to life. When you use it for good as God designed it, it is valuable and produces success. God says to cast down every imagination that goes against his knowledge. We have a choice as to how we think and there's no limit to how we can use our God-given imaginations, as long as those imaginations honor God and are part of His will.

In the Bible, Satan imagined himself being like the Most High and was cast out of heaven. Our thoughts can change our lives...

Scriptures:
2 Corinthians 10:5

We destroy arguments and every lofty opinion raised against the knowledge of God, and take every thought captive to obey Christ,

Genesis 6:5
The LORD saw that the wickedness of man was great in the earth, and that every intention of the thoughts of his heart was only evil continually.

Reflections: What do you imagine your life to be like in the next five years?

_____

_____

_____

Day 28

Don't let go

We must hold fast to God and never let go. Hold your position and don't lose sight of who God is in your life. Fix your eyes on him who is the author and finisher of your faith. If you have patience and wait on your heavenly father, he will give you the strength to finish the race.

We must trust that no matter where God leads us his love and grace will be enough. It might be hard, it might even be downright painful, but it will all be worth it! Don't give up. The storms of life may toss you to and fro, but don't wander from his side when they do.

If you are tightly secure to him and his promises, he will not fail you and the world cannot woo you from his presence. Holding fast starts with trusting in him.

Scriptures:
Isaiah: 40:31

But they who wait for the LORD shall renew their strength; they shall mount up with wings like eagles; they shall run and not be weary; they shall walk and not faint.

Psalm 91:14,15
"Because he holds fast to me in love, I will deliver him; I will protect him, because he knows my name. When he calls to me, I will answer him; I will be with him in trouble; I will rescue him and honor him.

Reflections: Are you anchored to the Lord?

_____

_____

_____

Day 29

Praise the Lord

Praise the Lord, for he is greatly to be praised. We shall have praise continually in our mouth for God who has been so good to us. We praise him because he woke us up this morning. We praise him for what he has given us, and for what he hasn't given us because he knows what's best for us.

Praise the Lord in the midst of your problems. Praise him and give him thanks for all he went through for you. Jesus has paid the price for our sins so all we should do is thank him for all he went through for us.

Joy comes when you praise him because you have faith that everything is going to be okay. God deserves all the glory and praise. When we offer praise to God, we acknowledge he is worthy of our attention and adoration. Let everything that has breath praise the Lord.

Scriptures:

Isaiah 25:1

O LORD, you are my God; I will exalt you; I will praise your name, for you have done wonderful things, plans formed of old, faithful and sure.

Psalm 150:6

Let everything that has breath praise the LORD! Praise the LORD!

Reflections: What do you do first thing in the morning?

_____

_____

_____

Day 30

Testify

Testify of God's goodness! Tell someone what God has done for you in your life. When you stand as a witness to God, you are standing as a witness of his miracles as well. Your testimony is setting people free from sickness, depression, anxiety, addiction, and worldly things.

I used to be a smoker but now I am smoke-free. God delivered me from that addiction. I thought I needed it to sleep and to feel calm, but I didn't. All I needed was God. He helped me have his peace that surpasses all understanding, and he gave me sleep because in his word he says he gives his beloved sleep (Psalms 127:2). God healed me from sickness, pain, and worldly desires. If he did it for me, he will do it for you as well.

Every test is for a testimony. Every mess is for a message. If Jesus had to go through trials, tribulation, and hatred, then who are we? He loves us so much he will not give you more than you can handle. Let the world know what God has done for you!

Scriptures:
Revelation 12:11
And they have conquered him by the blood of the Lamb and by the word of their testimony, for they loved not their lives even unto death.

John 21:24
This is the disciple who is bearing witness about these things, and who has written these things, and we know that his testimony is true.

Reflections: What has God done for you?

_____

_____

_____

Reflections

What have you learned from this 30-day devotional? How has your life changed in these 30 days?

My Prayer 🙏

Heavenly father, I come to you today thanking you for waking me up this morning. I think you, oh Lord, for the many blessings you have bestowed upon me. Thank you for your love, mercy and grace.

Lord, give me wisdom, knowledge, and understanding of who you are in my life. Please, Lord Jesus, forgive me for all unanointed words that proceed from my mouth. Bridle my tongue every day. Lord, may every limitation fall off of me. Lord, make me meek and slow to speak. Let the words of my mouth and the meditation of my heart be acceptable in thy sight.

Father, let my actions be aligned with your word. I am hungry to know about you. I desire your heart and your ways help me to be a light that shines brightly. Forgive me for all my sins, known and unknown, God help me to become all you have created me to be. Disconnect me from every wrong connection in my life. Break any ungodly relationships in Jesus' name.

Father, give me power and strength to do your will and embrace your purpose for my life. May I walk into the blessings you have for me this year. Increase my faith and take away any fear in my heart. Help me to focus my eyes, ears and heart on you Lord. Make a away for me and reveal my place of assignment. Cause me to be perpetual and fruitful in my family, job, home, and with my children.

Lord, by your spirit, mold me to become what you intended me to be. Father, break off any unforgiveness, hardship, frustration and limitation. May the grace over my life increase. Help me to grow physically and spiritually so I may serve your purpose on this earth. Heal me from any depression, anxiety, sickness, poverty, and any worldly things.

Father, set me apart for your glory. Give me the ability to remain in your presence and give me divine direction. Show me where my feet should be planted so I can prosper in everything that I do. In the mighty name of Jesus I pray, Amen.

Your Prayer 🙏

_____

_____

_____

Thank You

I would like to thank all my readers for taking the time out to read my devotional.

I ask that you give me honest feedback by leaving a rating or review.

May this devotional bless your life and help you become a better you.

Be sure to pass it on to your family and loved ones.

Remember our timeline is someone else's lifeline.

Any prayer requests or testimonies? I would love to hear how this devotional has changed your life.

Please contact me by email:

ebonyvazz@yahoo.com

Thanks For All Your Support

I dedicate this devotional to my brother, Michael Vaz, who was my inspiration and motivation, my hero, my oldest brother. He will always be missed!
Never forgotten.

Made in the USA
Columbia, SC
07 April 2025

607371b2-4dbf-4fd0-967a-748207bac056R01